50 Christmas Feast Recipes

By: Kelly Johnson

Table of Contents

- Classic Roast Turkey with Herb Butter
- Honey Glazed Ham with Cloves
- Garlic Rosemary Prime Rib Roast
- Cranberry Orange Glazed Duck
- Festive Stuffed Pork Loin
- Baked Maple Glazed Salmon
- Herb Roasted Cornish Hens
- Slow-Cooked Beef Brisket with Red Wine
- Traditional Christmas Goose
- Spiced Roast Leg of Lamb
- Buttery Garlic Mashed Potatoes
- Classic Sausage and Herb Stuffing
- Candied Sweet Potatoes with Pecans
- Creamy Baked Mac and Cheese
- Roasted Brussels Sprouts with Balsamic Glaze
- Parmesan Crusted Asparagus
- Green Bean Almondine
- Cheesy Scalloped Potatoes
- Honey Roasted Carrots with Thyme
- Warm Spiced Apple Cider
- Classic Eggnog with Nutmeg
- Cranberry Mimosa Cocktail
- Mulled Wine with Cinnamon and Cloves
- Pomegranate Christmas Punch
- Yorkshire Pudding with Pan Drippings
- Homemade Cranberry Sauce
- Festive Deviled Eggs with Paprika
- Garlic Butter Dinner Rolls
- Spinach and Pomegranate Salad
- Holiday Cheese and Charcuterie Board
- Christmas Fruitcake with Brandy
- Gingerbread Cookies with Royal Icing
- Classic Yule Log Cake (Bûche de Noël)
- Peppermint Bark with Dark Chocolate
- Cinnamon Sugar Baked Donuts

- Spiced Hot Chocolate with Marshmallows
- Sticky Toffee Pudding with Caramel Sauce
- Rum-Soaked Christmas Pudding
- Chocolate-Dipped Almond Biscotti
- Eggnog Cheesecake Bars
- Red Velvet Trifle with Cream Cheese Frosting
- Orange Cranberry Scones
- Candy Cane Chocolate Fudge
- Frosted Sugar Cookies
- Toasted Pecan Snowball Cookies
- White Chocolate Raspberry Cheesecake
- Gingerbread Spiced Bundt Cake
- Peppermint Mocha Cupcakes
- Maple Glazed Walnut Tart
- Hot Buttered Rum

Classic Roast Turkey with Herb Butter

Ingredients:

- 1 whole turkey (12-14 lbs)
- ½ cup unsalted butter, softened
- 2 tbsp fresh sage, chopped
- 2 tbsp fresh rosemary, chopped
- 2 tbsp fresh thyme, chopped
- 4 cloves garlic, minced
- Salt & black pepper to taste
- 1 lemon, halved
- 1 onion, quartered

Instructions:

1. Preheat oven to 325°F (165°C).
2. Pat turkey dry and season inside with salt and pepper.
3. Mix butter with herbs and garlic, rub under the skin and all over the turkey.
4. Stuff cavity with lemon and onion.
5. Roast for about 3-3.5 hours, basting occasionally, until internal temp reaches 165°F (75°C).

Honey Glazed Ham with Cloves

Ingredients:

- 1 (8-10 lb) bone-in ham
- ½ cup honey
- ¼ cup Dijon mustard
- ¼ cup brown sugar
- ½ tsp ground cloves
- ¼ tsp cinnamon
- Whole cloves for garnish

Instructions:

1. Preheat oven to 325°F (165°C).
2. Score ham in a diamond pattern and stud with whole cloves.
3. Mix honey, mustard, brown sugar, ground cloves, and cinnamon.
4. Brush over ham and bake for 2 hours, basting every 30 minutes.

Garlic Rosemary Prime Rib Roast

Ingredients:

- 1 (5-6 lb) bone-in prime rib
- 4 cloves garlic, minced
- 2 tbsp fresh rosemary, chopped
- 1 tbsp fresh thyme, chopped
- 2 tbsp olive oil
- 1 tbsp kosher salt
- 1 tsp black pepper

Instructions:

1. Preheat oven to 450°F (230°C).
2. Mix garlic, rosemary, thyme, oil, salt, and pepper into a paste.
3. Rub all over the roast and let sit at room temp for 30 minutes.
4. Roast for 20 minutes at 450°F, then lower to 325°F (165°C) and cook for 1.5-2 hours (medium-rare: 130°F).

Cranberry Orange Glazed Duck

Ingredients:

- 1 whole duck (4-5 lbs)
- ½ cup cranberry sauce
- ¼ cup orange juice
- 2 tbsp honey
- 1 tsp soy sauce
- 1 tsp grated orange zest
- Salt & black pepper

Instructions:

1. Preheat oven to 375°F (190°C).
2. Score duck skin, season with salt and pepper.
3. Roast for 90 minutes, draining fat occasionally.
4. Mix cranberry sauce, orange juice, honey, soy sauce, and zest.
5. Glaze duck in the last 20 minutes of roasting.

Festive Stuffed Pork Loin

Ingredients:

- 1 (3-4 lb) pork loin
- 1 cup breadcrumbs
- ½ cup dried cranberries
- ½ cup chopped pecans
- 1 apple, diced
- 1 tbsp fresh sage, chopped
- 1 tsp salt
- ½ tsp black pepper
- 2 tbsp olive oil

Instructions:

1. Preheat oven to 375°F (190°C).
2. Butterfly pork loin and season with salt and pepper.
3. Mix stuffing ingredients and spread evenly over pork.
4. Roll tightly, secure with kitchen twine.
5. Roast for 1.5 hours until internal temp reaches 145°F (63°C).

Baked Maple Glazed Salmon

Ingredients:

- 4 salmon fillets
- ¼ cup maple syrup
- 1 tbsp Dijon mustard
- 1 tbsp soy sauce
- 1 tsp garlic powder
- ½ tsp black pepper

Instructions:

1. Preheat oven to 400°F (200°C).
2. Mix glaze ingredients and brush over salmon.
3. Bake for 12-15 minutes.

Herb Roasted Cornish Hens

Ingredients:

- 2 Cornish hens
- 2 tbsp olive oil
- 1 tsp salt
- ½ tsp black pepper
- 1 tsp paprika
- 1 tsp dried thyme
- 2 cloves garlic, minced
- 1 lemon, quartered

Instructions:

1. Preheat oven to 375°F (190°C).
2. Rub hens with oil, season with spices.
3. Stuff with garlic and lemon.
4. Roast for 50-55 minutes.

Slow-Cooked Beef Brisket with Red Wine

Ingredients:

- 3-4 lb beef brisket
- 1 onion, sliced
- 3 cloves garlic, minced
- 1 cup red wine
- 2 cups beef broth
- 2 tbsp tomato paste
- 1 tbsp Worcestershire sauce
- 1 tsp thyme

Instructions:

1. Sear brisket in a hot pan for 3 minutes per side.
2. Place in a slow cooker with remaining ingredients.
3. Cook on low for 8 hours.

Traditional Christmas Goose

Ingredients:

- 1 whole goose (10-12 lbs)
- 2 tsp salt
- 1 tsp black pepper
- 1 tsp dried thyme
- 2 oranges, quartered
- 1 onion, quartered

Instructions:

1. Preheat oven to 350°F (175°C).
2. Season goose inside and out.
3. Stuff with oranges and onion.
4. Roast for 3-3.5 hours, draining fat as needed.

Spiced Roast Leg of Lamb

Ingredients:

- 1 (4-5 lb) leg of lamb
- 3 cloves garlic, minced
- 2 tbsp olive oil
- 1 tbsp fresh rosemary, chopped
- 1 tsp cumin
- 1 tsp smoked paprika
- 1 tsp salt
- ½ tsp black pepper

Instructions:

1. Preheat oven to 400°F (200°C).
2. Mix spices and rub all over lamb.
3. Roast for 20 minutes, then reduce to 325°F and cook for 1.5 hours (medium-rare: 130°F).

Buttery Garlic Mashed Potatoes

Ingredients:

- 3 lbs Yukon Gold potatoes, peeled and cubed
- 4 cloves garlic, minced
- ½ cup unsalted butter
- 1 cup heavy cream
- Salt & black pepper to taste
- 2 tbsp chopped parsley (optional)

Instructions:

1. Boil potatoes in salted water until fork-tender (about 15-20 min).
2. Drain and mash.
3. Heat butter, garlic, and cream until warm.
4. Mix into potatoes, season to taste, and serve with parsley garnish.

Classic Sausage and Herb Stuffing

Ingredients:

- 1 lb sausage, crumbled
- 1 loaf bread, cubed and dried
- 1 onion, diced
- 2 celery stalks, diced
- 2 cups chicken broth
- 2 tbsp fresh parsley, chopped
- 1 tbsp fresh sage, chopped
- 1 tbsp fresh thyme, chopped
- 2 tbsp butter
- Salt & black pepper

Instructions:

1. Preheat oven to 350°F (175°C).
2. Sauté sausage, onion, and celery in butter until soft.
3. Combine with bread cubes and herbs.
4. Mix in broth until moistened.
5. Bake for 30-35 min.

Candied Sweet Potatoes with Pecans

Ingredients:

- 4 sweet potatoes, peeled and sliced
- ½ cup brown sugar
- ¼ cup maple syrup
- 4 tbsp butter
- 1 tsp cinnamon
- ½ cup pecans, chopped

Instructions:

1. Preheat oven to 375°F (190°C).
2. Mix sugar, syrup, butter, and cinnamon.
3. Toss with sweet potatoes and bake for 45 min.
4. Sprinkle pecans on top in the last 10 min.

Creamy Baked Mac and Cheese

Ingredients:

- 16 oz elbow macaroni
- 4 tbsp butter
- ¼ cup flour
- 3 cups whole milk
- 2 cups shredded cheddar cheese
- 1 cup shredded mozzarella
- 1 cup shredded Parmesan
- 1 tsp salt
- ½ tsp black pepper
- ½ cup breadcrumbs (optional)

Instructions:

1. Cook pasta, drain, and set aside.
2. In a saucepan, melt butter, whisk in flour, and cook for 1 min.
3. Gradually add milk, then cheeses.
4. Mix with pasta and transfer to a baking dish.
5. Top with breadcrumbs and bake at 375°F for 20 min.

Roasted Brussels Sprouts with Balsamic Glaze

Ingredients:

- 1 lb Brussels sprouts, halved
- 2 tbsp olive oil
- 2 tbsp balsamic vinegar
- 1 tbsp honey
- Salt & black pepper

Instructions:

1. Preheat oven to 400°F (200°C).
2. Toss Brussels sprouts with oil, salt, and pepper.
3. Roast for 25-30 min.
4. Drizzle with balsamic and honey before serving.

Parmesan Crusted Asparagus

Ingredients:

- 1 bunch asparagus, trimmed
- 2 tbsp olive oil
- ¼ cup grated Parmesan
- ½ tsp garlic powder
- ½ tsp salt
- ¼ tsp black pepper

Instructions:

1. Preheat oven to 400°F (200°C).
2. Toss asparagus with oil and seasonings.
3. Arrange on a baking sheet, sprinkle Parmesan on top.
4. Roast for 12-15 min.

Green Bean Almondine

Ingredients:

- 1 lb green beans, trimmed
- 2 tbsp butter
- ½ cup sliced almonds
- 1 clove garlic, minced
- Juice of ½ lemon
- Salt & black pepper

Instructions:

1. Blanch green beans in boiling water for 3 min, then drain.
2. Sauté garlic and almonds in butter until golden.
3. Add green beans, season, and toss with lemon juice.

Cheesy Scalloped Potatoes

Ingredients:

- 3 lbs potatoes, thinly sliced
- 2 tbsp butter
- 2 tbsp flour
- 2 cups whole milk
- 1 cup shredded cheddar cheese
- ½ cup shredded Gruyère cheese
- ½ tsp salt
- ¼ tsp black pepper

Instructions:

1. Preheat oven to 375°F (190°C).
2. Make a roux with butter and flour, then slowly add milk.
3. Stir in cheeses until melted.
4. Layer potatoes in a baking dish, covering each layer with cheese sauce.
5. Bake for 50-60 min.

Honey Roasted Carrots with Thyme

Ingredients:

- 1 lb carrots, peeled and cut into sticks
- 2 tbsp honey
- 2 tbsp olive oil
- 1 tsp fresh thyme
- Salt & black pepper

Instructions:

1. Preheat oven to 400°F (200°C).
2. Toss carrots with honey, oil, and seasonings.
3. Roast for 25-30 min.

Warm Spiced Apple Cider

Ingredients:

- 8 cups apple cider
- 2 cinnamon sticks
- 4 whole cloves
- 2 star anise
- 1 orange, sliced
- 1-inch piece fresh ginger, sliced
- 2 tbsp brown sugar (optional)

Instructions:

1. In a large pot, combine cider, cinnamon, cloves, star anise, orange slices, and ginger.
2. Simmer on low for 30 minutes.
3. Strain and serve warm.

Classic Eggnog with Nutmeg

Ingredients:

- 4 cups whole milk
- 1 cup heavy cream
- 4 egg yolks
- ½ cup sugar
- 1 tsp vanilla extract
- ½ tsp ground nutmeg
- ¼ tsp cinnamon
- ½ cup bourbon or rum (optional)

Instructions:

1. Whisk egg yolks and sugar in a bowl until light.
2. Heat milk, cream, vanilla, nutmeg, and cinnamon in a saucepan until warm.
3. Slowly pour warm milk into egg mixture while whisking.
4. Return to heat and cook until thickened.
5. Remove from heat, add alcohol (if using), and chill.

Cranberry Mimosa Cocktail

Ingredients:

- 1 cup cranberry juice
- 1 bottle Champagne or Prosecco
- ¼ cup orange liqueur (e.g., Cointreau)
- Fresh cranberries for garnish

Instructions:

1. Fill glasses halfway with cranberry juice and orange liqueur.
2. Top with chilled Champagne.
3. Garnish with fresh cranberries.

Mulled Wine with Cinnamon and Cloves

Ingredients:

- 1 bottle red wine
- ¼ cup honey or sugar
- 2 cinnamon sticks
- 4 whole cloves
- 1 orange, sliced
- 1 star anise
- ¼ cup brandy (optional)

Instructions:

1. Heat wine, honey, and spices in a saucepan (do not boil).
2. Simmer for 15 minutes, then add brandy.
3. Serve warm with orange slices.

Pomegranate Christmas Punch

Ingredients:

- 2 cups pomegranate juice
- 1 cup orange juice
- 1 cup cranberry juice
- 2 cups sparkling water or ginger ale
- ½ cup vodka or rum (optional)
- Pomegranate seeds and orange slices for garnish

Instructions:

1. Mix all ingredients in a pitcher.
2. Chill before serving.
3. Serve over ice with garnish.

Yorkshire Pudding with Pan Drippings

Ingredients:

- 1 cup all-purpose flour
- 1 cup whole milk
- 2 large eggs
- ½ tsp salt
- ½ cup beef drippings or vegetable oil

Instructions:

1. Preheat oven to 425°F (220°C).
2. Whisk flour, milk, eggs, and salt until smooth.
3. Heat drippings in a muffin tin until sizzling.
4. Pour batter into the hot drippings and bake for 20-25 minutes.

Homemade Cranberry Sauce

Ingredients:

- 2 cups fresh cranberries
- ½ cup sugar
- ½ cup orange juice
- 1 tsp orange zest
- ½ tsp cinnamon

Instructions:

1. Simmer all ingredients in a saucepan for 15 minutes.
2. Stir until cranberries burst and sauce thickens.
3. Cool before serving.

Festive Deviled Eggs with Paprika

Ingredients:

- 6 large eggs
- ¼ cup mayonnaise
- 1 tsp Dijon mustard
- ½ tsp apple cider vinegar
- Salt & black pepper to taste
- Paprika & chives for garnish

Instructions:

1. Boil eggs for 10 minutes, then cool and peel.
2. Halve eggs and mix yolks with mayo, mustard, and vinegar.
3. Pipe mixture back into egg whites and sprinkle with paprika.

Garlic Butter Dinner Rolls

Ingredients:

- 12 dinner rolls
- 4 tbsp butter, melted
- 2 cloves garlic, minced
- 1 tbsp chopped parsley
- ¼ tsp salt

Instructions:

1. Preheat oven to 350°F (175°C).
2. Mix melted butter with garlic, parsley, and salt.
3. Brush over rolls and bake for 5-7 minutes.

Spinach and Pomegranate Salad

Ingredients:

- 4 cups baby spinach
- ½ cup pomegranate seeds
- ¼ cup crumbled feta cheese
- ¼ cup toasted pecans
- 2 tbsp balsamic vinaigrette

Instructions:

1. Toss all ingredients together in a large bowl.
2. Drizzle with balsamic vinaigrette before serving.

Holiday Cheese and Charcuterie Board

Ingredients:

- 3 types of cheese (Brie, sharp cheddar, blue cheese)
- 3 types of cured meats (salami, prosciutto, chorizo)
- Crackers and sliced baguette
- Grapes, figs, and dried apricots
- Mixed nuts (almonds, walnuts, pistachios)
- Honey and grainy mustard

Instructions:

1. Arrange cheeses and meats on a board.
2. Fill in gaps with fruit, nuts, and condiments.
3. Serve with crackers and bread.

Christmas Fruitcake with Brandy

Ingredients:

- 2 cups mixed dried fruit (raisins, currants, cherries)
- ½ cup brandy
- 1 cup butter, softened
- 1 cup brown sugar
- 3 eggs
- 2 cups all-purpose flour
- 1 tsp baking powder
- ½ tsp cinnamon
- ½ tsp nutmeg
- ¼ cup chopped walnuts

Instructions:

1. Soak dried fruit in brandy overnight.
2. Cream butter and sugar, then add eggs.
3. Mix in dry ingredients and fold in fruit and nuts.
4. Bake at 325°F (160°C) for 90 minutes.

Gingerbread Cookies with Royal Icing

Ingredients:

- 3 cups flour
- 1 tbsp ginger
- 1 tsp cinnamon
- ½ tsp nutmeg
- ½ tsp baking soda
- ½ cup butter
- ½ cup brown sugar
- ½ cup molasses
- 1 egg

Instructions:

1. Cream butter and sugar, then mix in molasses and egg.
2. Combine with dry ingredients.
3. Roll out and cut into shapes.
4. Bake at 350°F (175°C) for 10 minutes.
5. Decorate with royal icing.

Classic Yule Log Cake (Bûche de Noël)

Ingredients:

- 4 eggs
- ¾ cup sugar
- 1 tsp vanilla extract
- ¾ cup flour
- ¼ cup cocoa powder
- ½ tsp baking powder
- 1 cup heavy cream
- 2 tbsp powdered sugar
- 1 cup chocolate ganache

Instructions:

1. Beat eggs and sugar until fluffy, add vanilla.
2. Fold in dry ingredients and bake in a jelly roll pan.
3. Roll while warm, then unroll and fill with whipped cream.
4. Roll back up and coat with ganache.

Peppermint Bark with Dark Chocolate

Ingredients:

- 8 oz dark chocolate
- 8 oz white chocolate
- ½ tsp peppermint extract
- ½ cup crushed candy canes

Instructions:

1. Melt dark chocolate and spread on a baking sheet.
2. Chill until set, then melt white chocolate with peppermint extract and spread over dark chocolate.
3. Sprinkle with candy canes and chill until hardened.

Cinnamon Sugar Baked Donuts

Ingredients:

- 1 cup flour
- ½ cup sugar
- 1 tsp cinnamon
- ½ tsp nutmeg
- 1 tsp baking powder
- ½ cup milk
- 1 egg
- 2 tbsp melted butter

Instructions:

1. Mix all ingredients and pour into a greased donut pan.
2. Bake at 350°F (175°C) for 12 minutes.
3. Toss in cinnamon sugar while warm.

Spiced Hot Chocolate with Marshmallows

Ingredients:

- 2 cups milk
- ½ cup heavy cream
- 4 oz dark chocolate, chopped
- 2 tbsp cocoa powder
- 1 tbsp sugar
- ½ tsp cinnamon
- Pinch of cayenne (optional)

Instructions:

1. Heat milk and cream in a saucepan.
2. Whisk in chocolate, cocoa, sugar, and spices.
3. Serve with marshmallows.

Sticky Toffee Pudding with Caramel Sauce

Ingredients:

- 1 cup chopped dates
- 1 cup boiling water
- 1 tsp baking soda
- ½ cup butter
- ½ cup brown sugar
- 2 eggs
- 1 cup flour
- 1 tsp vanilla

Caramel Sauce:

- ½ cup butter
- ½ cup brown sugar
- ½ cup heavy cream

Instructions:

1. Soak dates in boiling water with baking soda.
2. Cream butter and sugar, then mix in eggs and vanilla.
3. Fold in flour and soaked dates, bake at 350°F (175°C) for 25 minutes.
4. Simmer caramel sauce ingredients and pour over cake.

Rum-Soaked Christmas Pudding

Ingredients:

- 1 cup mixed dried fruit
- ½ cup rum
- 1 cup flour
- ½ cup brown sugar
- ½ tsp cinnamon
- ½ tsp nutmeg
- ½ cup melted butter
- 2 eggs

Instructions:

1. Soak dried fruit in rum overnight.
2. Mix dry and wet ingredients, then fold in soaked fruit.
3. Steam for 2 hours in a pudding mold.
4. Serve with extra rum sauce.

Chocolate-Dipped Almond Biscotti

Ingredients:

- 2 cups all-purpose flour
- 1 tsp baking powder
- ½ tsp salt
- ¾ cup sugar
- 2 eggs
- 1 tsp vanilla extract
- 1 tsp almond extract
- ¾ cup chopped almonds
- 6 oz dark chocolate (for dipping)

Instructions:

1. Preheat oven to 350°F (175°C).
2. Mix flour, baking powder, and salt.
3. Beat eggs, sugar, vanilla, and almond extract.
4. Combine wet and dry ingredients, then fold in almonds.
5. Shape into a log and bake for 25 minutes.
6. Cool slightly, slice into biscotti, and bake for another 10 minutes.
7. Melt chocolate and dip biscotti ends, then let set.

Eggnog Cheesecake Bars

Ingredients:

- 1½ cups graham cracker crumbs
- ¼ cup melted butter
- 16 oz cream cheese, softened
- ½ cup sugar
- 2 eggs
- ½ cup eggnog
- ½ tsp nutmeg
- 1 tsp vanilla extract

Instructions:

1. Preheat oven to 325°F (160°C).
2. Mix graham cracker crumbs with melted butter and press into a pan.
3. Beat cream cheese, sugar, and eggs until smooth.
4. Mix in eggnog, nutmeg, and vanilla.
5. Pour over crust and bake for 30 minutes.
6. Cool, refrigerate, then slice into bars.

Red Velvet Trifle with Cream Cheese Frosting

Ingredients:

- 1 red velvet cake (baked and cooled)
- 8 oz cream cheese, softened
- 1 cup powdered sugar
- 1 tsp vanilla extract
- 1½ cups heavy whipping cream
- ½ cup crushed candy canes (optional)

Instructions:

1. Beat cream cheese, powdered sugar, and vanilla until smooth.
2. Whip heavy cream until stiff peaks form, then fold into cream cheese mixture.
3. Crumble red velvet cake and layer with frosting in a trifle dish.
4. Top with crushed candy canes if desired.

Orange Cranberry Scones

Ingredients:

- 2 cups all-purpose flour
- ¼ cup sugar
- 2 tsp baking powder
- ½ tsp salt
- ½ cup cold butter, cubed
- ½ cup dried cranberries
- Zest of 1 orange
- ½ cup heavy cream
- 1 egg
- 1 tsp vanilla extract

Instructions:

1. Preheat oven to 400°F (200°C).
2. Mix flour, sugar, baking powder, and salt.
3. Cut in butter until mixture is crumbly.
4. Stir in cranberries and orange zest.
5. Mix cream, egg, and vanilla, then fold into the dough.
6. Shape into a circle, cut into wedges, and bake for 15 minutes.

Candy Cane Chocolate Fudge

Ingredients:

- 2 cups semi-sweet chocolate chips
- 1 can sweetened condensed milk
- 1 tsp vanilla extract
- ½ cup crushed candy canes

Instructions:

1. Melt chocolate chips with condensed milk over low heat.
2. Stir in vanilla and pour into a lined pan.
3. Sprinkle crushed candy canes on top.
4. Chill for 2 hours, then cut into squares.

Frosted Sugar Cookies

Ingredients:

- 2½ cups all-purpose flour
- 1 tsp baking powder
- ½ tsp salt
- ¾ cup butter, softened
- ¾ cup sugar
- 1 egg
- 1 tsp vanilla extract

For Frosting:

- 2 cups powdered sugar
- 2 tbsp milk
- 1 tsp vanilla
- Food coloring (optional)

Instructions:

1. Preheat oven to 350°F (175°C).
2. Cream butter and sugar, then mix in egg and vanilla.
3. Gradually add flour, baking powder, and salt.
4. Roll out dough, cut into shapes, and bake for 8-10 minutes.
5. Mix frosting ingredients and decorate cooled cookies.

Toasted Pecan Snowball Cookies

Ingredients:

- 1 cup unsalted butter, softened
- ½ cup powdered sugar
- 1 tsp vanilla extract
- 2 cups all-purpose flour
- 1 cup toasted pecans, finely chopped
- ¼ tsp salt
- 1 cup powdered sugar (for rolling)

Instructions:

1. Preheat oven to 350°F (175°C).
2. Beat butter, powdered sugar, and vanilla until creamy.
3. Mix in flour, salt, and pecans until dough forms.
4. Roll dough into 1-inch balls and place on a baking sheet.
5. Bake for 12-15 minutes, until lightly golden.
6. Cool slightly, then roll in powdered sugar.

White Chocolate Raspberry Cheesecake

Ingredients:

Crust:

- 1½ cups graham cracker crumbs
- ¼ cup melted butter
- ¼ cup sugar

Filling:

- 24 oz cream cheese, softened
- ¾ cup sugar
- 3 eggs
- 1 tsp vanilla extract
- 6 oz white chocolate, melted
- ½ cup raspberry preserves

Instructions:

1. Preheat oven to 325°F (160°C).
2. Mix crust ingredients, press into a springform pan, and bake for 10 minutes.
3. Beat cream cheese and sugar until smooth.
4. Add eggs one at a time, then mix in vanilla and melted white chocolate.
5. Pour into crust, swirl raspberry preserves on top.
6. Bake for 45-50 minutes, then chill for 4 hours before serving.

Gingerbread Spiced Bundt Cake

Ingredients:

- 2½ cups all-purpose flour
- 1 tsp baking soda
- ½ tsp salt
- 1 tbsp ground ginger
- 1 tsp cinnamon
- ½ tsp nutmeg
- ½ cup unsalted butter, softened
- ¾ cup brown sugar
- ½ cup molasses
- 2 eggs
- 1 cup buttermilk

Instructions:

1. Preheat oven to 350°F (175°C).
2. Whisk flour, baking soda, salt, and spices.
3. Beat butter and brown sugar until fluffy.
4. Add molasses and eggs, then alternate adding dry ingredients and buttermilk.
5. Pour into a greased bundt pan and bake for 40-45 minutes.
6. Let cool, then dust with powdered sugar or drizzle with icing.

Peppermint Mocha Cupcakes

Ingredients:

- 1 cup all-purpose flour
- ½ cup cocoa powder
- 1 tsp baking powder
- ½ tsp salt
- ½ cup hot brewed coffee
- ½ cup milk
- ½ cup unsalted butter, softened
- ¾ cup sugar
- 1 egg
- 1 tsp vanilla extract
- ½ tsp peppermint extract

Frosting:

- 1 cup unsalted butter, softened
- 2 cups powdered sugar
- 2 tbsp cocoa powder
- 1 tsp vanilla extract
- ½ tsp peppermint extract
- 2 tbsp heavy cream
- Crushed candy canes (for topping)

Instructions:

1. Preheat oven to 350°F (175°C).
2. Whisk flour, cocoa powder, baking powder, and salt.
3. Beat butter and sugar, add egg and extracts.
4. Alternate adding dry ingredients and milk/coffee.
5. Fill cupcake liners and bake for 18-20 minutes.
6. For frosting, beat butter, powdered sugar, cocoa, extracts, and cream until fluffy.
7. Pipe onto cooled cupcakes and top with crushed candy canes.

Maple Glazed Walnut Tart

Ingredients:

- 1½ cups all-purpose flour
- ½ cup cold butter, cubed
- ¼ cup sugar
- 1 egg yolk
- 2 tbsp cold water

Filling:

- 1 cup walnuts, chopped
- ½ cup maple syrup
- ¼ cup brown sugar
- 2 eggs
- ½ tsp cinnamon
- ¼ cup melted butter

Instructions:

1. Preheat oven to 350°F (175°C).
2. Mix flour, sugar, and butter until crumbly, then add yolk and water.
3. Press into a tart pan and chill for 30 minutes.
4. Whisk filling ingredients and pour into crust.
5. Bake for 30-35 minutes, until set.
6. Cool and drizzle with extra maple syrup.

Hot Buttered Rum

Ingredients:

- ½ cup unsalted butter, softened
- ½ cup brown sugar
- 1 tsp cinnamon
- ½ tsp nutmeg
- ¼ tsp cloves
- 1 pinch salt
- 2 cups boiling water
- ½ cup dark rum

Instructions:

1. Mix butter, sugar, and spices into a smooth paste.
2. Add 1 tbsp of mixture to a mug, pour in boiling water and stir.
3. Add dark rum, stir again, and serve warm.

www.ingramcontent.com/pod-product-compliance
Lightning Source LLC
LaVergne TN
LVHW081333060526
838201LV00055B/2616